KWANZAA
KARAMU

KWANZAA
COOKING AND CRAFTS

KARAMU
FOR A KWANZAA FEAST

APRIL A. BRADY

Illustrations by Barbara Knutson
Photographs by Robert L. and Diane Wolfe

Additional recipes by Cheryl Davidson Kaufman, Constance
Nabwire, Bertha Vining Montgomery, and Marcia Vaughan

CAROLRHODA BOOKS, INC./MINNEAPOLIS

*To my mother, Carole, and my sister, Chandra, who helped
me realize that the strength of an African-American woman
is not only inherited but acquired, and to my dear friends
Carolyn and Troy for believing in me and encouraging me to
continue writing. Thanks to them and to my Savior.—A.A.B.*

*Artist's note: The designs on the front cover of this book are based on
Tanzanian wood carvings that symbolize working together to build
communities and nations.*

Special thanks to Beeswax Candles, Etcetera,
Minneapolis, Minnesota.

This book is available in two editions:
Library binding by Carolrhoda Books, Inc.
Soft cover by First Avenue Editions c/o The Lerner Group
241 First Avenue North, Minneapolis, MN 55401

Library of Congress Cataloging-in-Publication Data
Brady, April A.
  Kwanzaa karamu : cooking and crafts for a Kwanzaa feast / April A.
Brady ; illustrations by Barbara Knutson ; photographs by Robert L. and
Diane Wolfe ; additional recipes by Cheryl Davidson Kaufman, Constance
Nabwire, Bertha Vining Montgomery, and Marcia Vaughan.
     p. cm.
  Includes index.
  ISBN 0-87614-842-9 (lib. bdg.) 0-87614-633-7 (pbk.)
  1. Afro-American cookery—Juvenile literature. 2. Holiday cookery—
United States—Juvenile literature. 3. Kwanzaa—Juvenile literature. 4.
Kwanzaa decorations—Juvenile literature. 5. Handicraft—Juvenile litera-
ture. [1. Kwanzaa. 2. Afro-American cookery. 3. Cookery. 4. Kwanzaa
decorations. 5. Handicraft.] I. Knutson, Barbara, ill. II. Title.
Tx715.B8144 1995
641.59'296073—dc20   94-20871
                                                      CIP
                                                      AC

Manufactured in the United States of America
2 3 4 5 6 7 – JR – 01 00 99 98 97 96

Contents

Editor's Note 6

All About Kwanzaa 7

Recipes 21
Cooking Smart 22
   Before You Cook 22
   While You Cook 22
   After You Cook 23
   Cooking Terms 23
Side Dishes & Breads 25
   Ants-on-a-Log 25
   Hush Puppies 26
   Cornmeal and Wheat Corn Bread 27
   Chapatis 28
Soups 29
   Callaloo 29
   Pick-a-Pepper Soup 30
Main Dishes 33
   Deep-Fried Catfish 33
   Red Beans and Rice 34
   Hopping John 35
   Luku 37
   Meat Curry 38
   Betty's Browned-Down Chicken 39

Vegetables 41
   Mixed Salad Greens
     with Orange-Lemon Dressing 41
   Honey-Glazed Sweet Potatoes 42
   Steamed Kale 43
Desserts 45
   Chandra's Peach Cobbler 45
   Baked Plantain on the Shell 46
   Sweet Balls 47

Crafts 49
   Before You Begin 49
   Mkeka 50
   Kinara Tapestry 52
   African Bowl or Mask 55
   African Headdress and Skirt 58

Nguzo Saba: The Seven Principles 60
Words for Kwanzaa 61
Index 62
Metric Conversion Chart 63
About the Author 64

Editor's Note

Kwanzaa Karamu *is divided into three parts. In the first part, April A. Brady shares her impressions of Kwanzaa, the holiday celebration of African and African-American cultures. Getting together to share good food is a big part of Kwanzaa, so the second part of this book is packed with recipes from Africa, the Caribbean, and the United States. In the last part of this book, you'll find craft and decorating ideas to help make your next Kwanzaa celebration the best ever. You'll also find a pronunciation key for new words in the section called "Words for Kwanzaa" on page 61.*

All About KWANZAA

 I would like to pass on to you what has been given to me, our history. The tales of the history of African Americans warm my heart and my mind like a fire burning. This flame will burn forever. It will never go out as long as you carry it into your life and into your children's lives. So listen as I tell the story of Kwanzaa.

Kwanzaa is an African-American holiday. It was created in 1966 by Dr. Maulana Karenga. We celebrate Kwanzaa over seven days, from December 26 through January 1. Each family has its own way of celebrating Kwanzaa, but all families follow the basic ideas or principles of Kwanzaa developed by Dr. Karenga.

Dr. Karenga is now the director of the African-American Cultural Center in Los Angeles, California. He teaches classes and directs the department of black studies at California State University in Long Beach. But, back in 1966, Karenga was a young scholar and philosopher studying the history of Africa and African societies.

All African Americans are descendants of the people of Africa. Africa is the second largest continent on earth, and it is made up of many countries and cultures. In 1966, Africa's great history wasn't being taught in most American schools. Karenga wanted to share all that he had learned about his culture.

During his studies, Karenga was also working hand in hand with others to help build Watts, an African-American community in Los Angeles. It was his work in African-American neighborhoods that inspired him to create Kwanzaa.

The first celebration began with a few hundred people. Since that first Kwanzaa, Maulana and his wife, Tiamoyo, have been involved in celebrations all over the world.

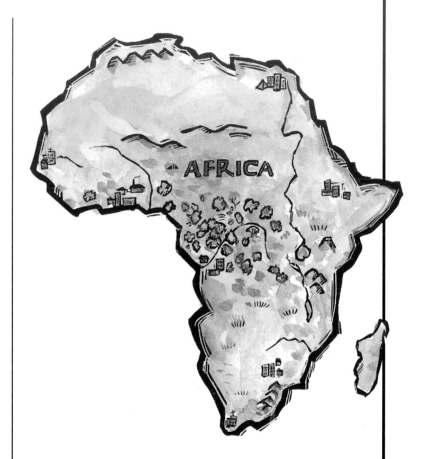

Kwanzaa is a celebration of both Africa and America, of the past and present and future of our people. Dr. Karenga created Kwanzaa to teach African Americans the history of our culture and to encourage us to turn to our history for support.

We can see this history in the African-American flag, or bendera. Each color in the bendera is a symbol, something that stands for an idea. Black stands for the color of our people. The red band stands for our struggle, for the blood lost by our ancestors in our continuing quest for freedom. Green symbolizes the land of Africa, its green hills and our constant hope for the future. These colors and the ideas behind them are all part of Kwanzaa.

Before the celebration starts, we must gather the seven symbols of Kwanzaa. First we place on the table the mkeka, a handwoven mat. The mkeka reminds us of a

time in our history when all things were made by hand and showed our talent and creativity.

The word *mkeka* comes from the Swahili or Kiswahili language. This language is spoken in the eastern regions of Africa. When Dr. Karenga created Kwanzaa, he used this and other Swahili words to remind us of Africa.

Next we place the kinara, or candleholder, on the table. The kinara symbolizes our ancestors. Seven candles, called the mishumaa saba, are placed in the candleholder. Three green candles stand on the right, three red candles on the left, and one black candle in the center. As in the bendera, the colors represent three parts of African-American culture—black for our people, red for our struggle, and green for our future.

Also placed on the table are the mazao, or fruits and vegetables. We display the mazao in a bowl to symbolize the African harvest. Along with the mazao, we put muhindi, or ears of corn, on the table. The muhindi stand for children and their importance to the future and success of the family. One ear of corn is placed on the mkeka for each child in the family. If there are no children, an ear of corn is set out to stand for all African-American children.

The muhindi remind us that children are the future of our people.

The kikombe cha umoja, or unity cup, also goes on the mkeka. Everyone who takes part in the celebration will drink from this cup as a way of strengthening unity in the family and community.

The last symbols placed on the mkeka are the zawadi, or gifts. Normally these gifts are passed down from the elders to the children. Many parents give children gifts that have been passed down from their own parents. Some of these gifts were received when they were small children celebrating Kwanzaa years ago.

In some families, traditions are changing. Children are encouraged to create gifts for the older members of the family to express their respect and love. It's easy to bring this tradition into your Kwanzaa celebration. Zawadi can be poems you recite, stories you write about your family, or pictures you draw. Wherever your creativity lies—in singing, dancing, writing, or drawing—give this as your zawadi. The gifts are presented on the sixth day of Kwanzaa.

Once the mkeka, kinara, mishumaa saba, mazao, muhindi, kikombe cha umoja, and zawadi are all on the table, it's time to celebrate. On December 26, Kwanzaa begins. *Kwanzaa* is a Swahili word which means the first fruits of harvest. During those early harvests, our African ancestors worked hard. With the help of the sun, our people were able to harvest plenty of food to feed us all. Even though few African Americans today work harvesting crops, we join together at Kwanzaa time to celebrate a harvest of family, friends, and culture.

Kwanzaa isn't a religious holiday or an alternative to Christmas. So it doesn't matter if you are Catholic, Baptist, Methodist, or atheist—you can celebrate Kwanzaa. Kwanzaa helps us strengthen the bond between all our people, bringing us closer as we share in the celebration.

No matter what our religion may be, during Kwanzaa we join together. It's a time to celebrate life, family, love, friends, and all those who have given richness and essence to our lives. It's also the time for observing the seven principles of Kwanzaa, known as the nguzo saba. The nguzo saba were created by Dr. Karenga. They tell us about the values behind Kwanzaa. They define how and why we celebrate the holiday.

The word *nguzo* means principles, and *saba* means seven. There is a principle for each of the seven days of Kwanzaa: umoja, kujichagulia, ujima, ujamaa, nia, kuumba, and imani. On each day of Kwanzaa, we light one of the candles in the kinara and observe one of the nguzo saba.

The first principle of Kwanzaa is umoja, the unity of all African Americans. We celebrate umoja on the first day of Kwanzaa, December 26. The first candle lit is the black candle. The person lighting the candle must tell why it is being lit. That person opens the celebration by talking about what umoja, or unity, means.

This is what umoja means to me: It means that we must work to come together as a family of one. At Kwanzaa time, we invite those who are alone, who don't have children, or who have lost members of their family to join us. In celebration of umoja, we gather as one, sharing the feeling of strength that comes when we are together. We open our hearts and our homes to friends and neighbors.

honor those who have died. Then the leader drinks from the cup, lifts it up high, and shouts, "Harambee!" *Harambee* means "let's all pull together, let's work together as a family and community." We all say "Harambee!" seven times, once for each principle of Kwanzaa. Then each person takes a sip from the cup. Each day when we celebrate one of the nguzo saba, we drink from the cup again to reinforce the principle.

After we talk about umoja, the ceremony continues. We remember family members who have died. We celebrate, too, the value of unity in the family. The kikombe cha umoja, or unity cup, is filled with juice or water. The same person who starts the Kwanzaa celebration now pours some of the juice or water into a large bowl to

The second principle is kujichagulia, or self-determination. Kujichagulia is celebrated on the second day of Kwanzaa. This is when we relight the black candle and light the red candle closest to the center. Everyone shares ideas about kujichagulia. We talk about what we are presently doing or what we want to do for ourselves and for

others. Just as on the first night, the person who lights the candle leads the celebration. And as we celebrate kujichagulia, we drink from the unity cup again.

For me, kujichagulia means having the self-discipline and the desire to be the very best I can be. Think about it this way: When your parents ask you to do something for them, take the time to do your best. When you set a goal for yourself—to do better in school or to be a kinder friend— believe that your goal is possible and then work toward making it happen. Don't let anyone else tell you what your goals should be.

We celebrate ujima on the third day of Kwanzaa, December 28. All the candles from the previous days are lit, along with the green candle closest to the center.

To me, ujima is the most important of the nguzo saba, because it means working together to achieve success. To achieve any goal in life requires the help of another person. No one goes through life on his or her own. To win a game, the whole team has to work together. To build a proud neighborhood, we must work closely with our neighbors. To be a strong family, we must all—parents, brothers, and sisters—support each other in all we do.

That's practicing ujima. When one in a family or community succeeds, then we all succeed. When we work together to build up our families and communities, our pride in ourselves grows. This pride is reflected in everything we want to achieve and in everything we succeed in doing.

The fourth principle is ujamaa, sharing work and sharing the profit from that work as a family and a community. On this day, we light the fourth candle, a red one. Now there are one black, one green, and two red candles burning to celebrate the four days of

Kwanzaa. This is the day when everyone talks about work and sharing, about building our own stores, shops, and businesses. When we build these things, we are also building our future.

The fifth principle is nia, or purpose. Nia is celebrated on December 30. On this night, we light the fifth candle, a green one. Then it's time to think and talk about nia.

Nia is the principle that stands behind all the others. When we come together (umoja), when we decide to do our best (kujichagu-lia), when we work together (ujima), and we share our work and our profits (ujamaa), we have a larger purpose or goal. When we talk about our purpose, or nia, we talk about our future. We talk about setting goals for the future

that will help our family, our community, and ourselves.

Each of us shares our goals as we drink from the kikombe cha umoja. While remembering family members who have passed away, we talk about their achievements. And we celebrate the successes of other African Americans who enrich our lives. When we have nia, we have pride in our ancestors, in ourselves, and in the past and future of African Americans.

Kuumba, or creativity, is celebrated on the sixth day of Kwanzaa, which is also New Year's Eve. The first five candles are lit along with the sixth candle, a red one. Then it's time for the fun to begin.

On the sixth day, we celebrate with a great feast called the karamu. For the first five days of Kwanzaa, our family comes together each night for the ceremony. But on this day, other families and special friends sometimes join us. As people come through the door, we invite them to share in all we have to give. We greet our guests with a hug or a kind word to show them our love and gratitude. Everyone brings food to share, and we all try to find room for it in the kitchen, on the mkeka, or wherever it will fit!

For the karamu, we decorate the room in black, red, and green. And we put a big mkeka on the floor. The candleholder, vegetables, basket of fruit, cup, corn, and gifts are all placed on the mat. As we gather around the mkeka, we talk about the things we are doing by ourselves and as a group to bring kuumba, or creativity, into our homes and neighborhoods and communities.

On the sixth day, we use our creativity in the kitchen to make wonderful foods. We use our talents to create crafts, play music, or dance with each other, because this is a special day. Everyone contributes something he or she has made to the festivities. Creating only makes life more beautiful, and that's what kuumba is all about.

As we drink from the cup, we share our stories. Many are tales of great people, African Americans who are now our heroes. When we all have had a chance to speak, we come together to eat.

After the feast, there is more music and dancing and celebrating. It's also time for giving the zawadi. Once everyone has opened the gifts, the celebration continues late into the night with still more music and laughter.

When kuumba ends at midnight on December 31, imani begins. It is the new year and time for a new beginning. The last candle is lit, and now all of the mishumaa saba are burning. We come together around the kinara to talk about imani, or faith.

On this last day of Kwanzaa, we talk about what we believe in, we talk about our faith, and we talk about our belief in ourselves and in our parents. To me, imani means believing. Many of us want to believe in something greater than ourselves. We may learn about the books of the Bible, about the Koran, or about the Torah. Whatever our religion, when we have imani, we have faith in the future.

As the candles of Kwanzaa burn brightly, we talk about the year just ended and about our plans for the days ahead. We pass the unity cup for the last time to family and friends. Each of us drinks from the cup before shouting one last "Harambee!"

Even though Kwanzaa has ended, we can remember its lessons year round. As we start each new day, we can make the nguzo saba a part of our lives. Making the seven principles of Kwanzaa part of your life on a daily basis may seem hard, but it isn't. How will you know if you are using the principles? With each new day, ask yourself these questions:

♦ Have I worked to bring people together? Umoja unites each of us in our feelings and ideas.
♦ Do I have the determination to get the most out of my life?

At the end of the day, think about how much kujichagulia you've shown. Think about what you have achieved and about the work you still must do. Set goals and work to meet them.

♦ How am I using my talents and skills to help those who need it? The principle of ujima helps us to help others. If you do well in school, why not help others who have a hard time with certain classes? If you are good in sports, work to make your team better. We can all use what we do well to help others do well.

♦ Am I helping out with the work to be done at home or in the community? Ujamaa means sharing all we have to give and knowing that each of us will gain as we live. It also means sharing our work. So if there's a job to be done, pitch in!

♦ Do I have a sense of purpose, or a larger goal? Never forget that your nia, or purpose, is important to the success of our people.

♦ Am I using my creativity to make my neighborhood and home more beautiful? Whatever your talent, share it! Kuumba makes life beautiful and more meaningful.

♦ Do I have faith in myself, in my parents, and in my community? Imani, or faith, makes us strong. It helps us keep our commitment, every day, to the nguzo saba.

When we bring the principles of Kwanzaa into our daily lives, we show our faith in our people, our struggle, and our culture—just as Dr. Karenga intended.

RECIPES

 Cooking is a sacred activity. It celebrates the pleasures of food and love. When we prepare a meal and share it with family and friends, we are taking part in traditions that connect us all as human beings. The kitchen has always been a central place within the African-American family. It is in the kitchen that my love for food first began. I can remember as a small child helping my mother prepare meals and special dishes that had been served in our family for generations.

Since the first Kwanzaa in 1966, our people have come together to celebrate, with food, the feast of life. Each family, whether a family of one or many, contributes a dish of food—whatever they can afford—to share with all. Food is the simple gift of life, which allows us to show how much we love and appreciate each other.

Betty's browned-down chicken will add the tangy taste of the Caribbean to your karamu. You'll find this recipe on page 39.

Cooking Smart

Before You Cook

♦ Get yourself ready. If you have long hair, tie it back to keep it out of the food, away from flames, and out of your way. Roll up your sleeves and put on an apron. Be sure to wash your hands well with soap.

♦ Read through the entire recipe and assemble all of the ingredients. It's no fun to find out halfway through a recipe that you're out of eggs.

♦ Choose a recipe that fits your skills. Go through the recipe with an adult helper and decide which steps you can perform yourself and which you'll need help with. If you're a beginning cook, you might want to start with recipes like ants-on-a-log or the mixed salad greens.

While You Cook

♦ Remember that raw meat and eggs can contain dangerous bacteria. Wash your hands and any utensils or cutting boards you've used after handling these raw foods. Never put cooked meat on an unwashed plate that has held raw meat. Any dough that contains raw eggs isn't safe to eat until it's cooked.

♦ Keep cold foods in the refrigerator until you need them.

♦ Wash fruits and vegetables thoroughly before using them.

♦ Turn pot handles to the back of the stove so the pots won't be knocked off accidentally. When you are taking the lid off a hot pan, always keep the opening away from your face so the steam won't burn you.

♦ Use a pot holder when handling hot pans.

♦ Always turn off the stove or oven as soon as you're done.
♦ Don't cut up food in your hand. Use a cutting board.
♦ Carry knives point down.
♦ Be careful when opening cans. The edges of the lids are very sharp.
♦ Don't save the mess for the end. Try to clean up as you go along.

After You Cook

♦ Once you've finished cooking, be sure to store your leftover food in the refrigerator if it contains any ingredients that might spoil.
♦ Be a courteous cook: Clean up your mess. Leave the kitchen looking as clean as (or cleaner than) you found it.

Cooking Terms

beat: To stir rapidly in a circular motion

boil: To heat a liquid over high heat until bubbles form and rise rapidly to the surface

brown: To cook food quickly in fat over high heat so that the surface turns an even brown

grease: To coat with a thin layer of butter, margarine, or shortening

knead: To work dough by pressing it with the palms, pushing it outward, and then pressing it over on itself

preheat: To allow an oven to heat up to a certain temperature

sauté: To fry quickly over high heat in oil or fat, stirring or turning the food to prevent burning

simmer: To cook over low heat in liquid kept just below its boiling point. Bubbles may occasionally rise to the surface.

Traditional hopping John (upper left) goes well with crispy hush puppies (bottom). For a quick appetizer, try ants-on-a-log (center). The recipe for hopping John is on page 35, while you'll find the recipe for hush puppies on page 26.

SIDE DISHES & BREADS
Ants-on-a-Log
United States

Easy to make and healthy too, these appetizers are welcome at any feast. (Recipe by Marcia Vaughan)

4   stalks celery
    peanut butter
    raisins

1. Wash and dry celery stalks. Cut each stalk into 3-inch-long pieces.
2. Spread peanut butter along the groove of each piece of celery.
3. Dot with raisins.
4. Arrange "logs" on a plate.

Serves 4

HOW TO MAKE PEANUT BUTTER

1   cup shelled peanuts
1½ tablespoons peanut oil
½   teaspoon salt

1. Put peanuts in bowl of a food processor or blender. Blend for about 1 minute, until peanuts are crushed into a paste.
2. Stir in oil and salt.
3. Store in a covered container and refrigerate. Note: If peanuts and oil separate, simply stir to mix. For crunchy peanut butter, blend peanuts for a shorter time.

Hush Puppies
United States

How did hush puppies get their name? According to legend, the dish was invented by black plantation cooks who were frying up fish. Because of the heat, most cooking was done outdoors. To keep the local dogs at bay, one cook took some fish batter, dropped it in the oil, and threw the puffed ball to the dogs, yelling, "Hush, puppies!" (Recipe by Marcia Vaughan)

1¾ cups white or yellow cornmeal
¼ cup all-purpose flour
2 teaspoons baking powder
¼ teaspoon ground thyme
¼ teaspoon salt
1 cup milk
2 eggs, beaten
½ onion, finely chopped
   vegetable oil for frying

1. Stir together cornmeal, flour, baking powder, thyme, and salt in a large mixing bowl.

2. Add the milk, eggs, and onion. Beat well with a large spoon. The mixture should be the consistency of pancake batter.

3. Heat ½ inch of oil in an electric skillet to 375° or use a heavy skillet over high heat.

4. Carefully drop the batter into the hot oil in level tablespoonfuls. Be careful not to splatter the hot oil. Fry 1 or 2 minutes, or until golden brown on each side, turning the hush puppies with a spatula. Depending on the size of your pan, you may be able to cook 3 or 4 hush puppies at a time.

5. Carefully lift the hush puppies from the hot oil with a slotted spoon. Drain on paper towels and serve warm.

Makes 32 hush puppies

Cornmeal and Wheat Corn Bread

United States

When I was a child, most meals were accompanied by bread, but any meal with beans or greens always had to have corn bread.—A.A.B.

1	tablespoon butter or margarine
1½	cups whole wheat flour
5	teaspoons baking powder
¾	teaspoon cinnamon
1	cup yellow cornmeal
½	cup (1 stick) butter or margarine, softened
⅔	cup brown sugar, packed tightly in measuring cup
3	eggs
3	tablespoons fresh-squeezed lemon juice
1	cup 2% or skim milk

1. Preheat oven to 350°. Use 1 tablespoon butter or margarine to grease 2 loaf pans. Set aside.
2. In a medium bowl, combine flour, baking powder, and cinnamon. Mix well, then add cornmeal and mix again.
3. In a large bowl, beat butter until smooth. Beat in sugar, then add eggs and lemon juice. Continue beating until mixture is smooth and fluffy.
4. While beating, add flour mixture and milk a little at a time. Mix until well blended.
5. Spoon batter into loaf pans and bake for 35 to 40 minutes, or until a fork inserted in the center comes out clean. Allow loaves to cool in their pans for 5 minutes. Carefully remove and place on a cooling rack. Slice and serve when cool.

Makes 2 loaves

Chapatis
Kenya, Tanzania, Uganda

This thin fried bread is delicious with butter or covered with jam. Or use chapatis instead of silverware to dish up bites of meat curry, shown on page 36. (Recipe by Constance Nabwire and Bertha Vining Montgomery)

½ teaspoon salt
3 cups unbleached
   all-purpose flour
¾ cup plus 1 to 3
   tablespoons vegetable oil
¾ to 1 cup water

1. In a large bowl, combine salt and 2½ cups flour. Add ¾ cup oil and mix well. Add water little by little, stirring after each addition, until dough is soft. Knead dough in bowl for 5 to 10 minutes.
2. Sprinkle about ¼ cup flour on a flat surface. Take a 2-inch ball of dough and, with a floured rolling pin, roll out into a ⅛-inch-thick circle the size of a saucer. Repeat with remaining dough, sprinkling flat surface with flour if dough sticks.
3. Heat 1 tablespoon oil over medium-high heat for 1 minute. Fry chapatis 3 to 5 minutes per side or until brown.
4. Remove from pan and let drain on paper towels. Fry remaining chapatis, adding more oil if necessary.
5. Serve immediately or place in a covered container until ready to serve.

Makes 6 chapatis

SOUPS
Callaloo
Caribbean Islands

This soup is traditionally made with callaloo greens, which were introduced to the Caribbean by Africans. In this recipe, spinach is used instead. (Recipe by Cheryl Davidson Kaufman)

4	tablespoons butter or margarine
1	small onion, chopped
1	clove garlic, peeled and chopped
3	cups chicken broth
½	cup coconut milk, fresh or canned, unsweetened
1	medium potato, peeled and chopped
1	teaspoon salt
1½	teaspoons black pepper
¾	pound fresh spinach with stems removed, chopped
½	pound cooked crabmeat
	paprika

1. In a large kettle, melt butter over medium-high heat. Add onions and garlic and sauté for about 5 minutes or until onion is transparent.

2. Add chicken broth, coconut milk, potato, salt, and pepper to kettle and stir well. Bring to a boil over high heat.

3. Reduce heat to low and cover, leaving cover slightly ajar. Simmer for 15 minutes or until potato can be easily pierced with a fork.

4. Add spinach and simmer, uncovered, for 10 minutes or until spinach is tender.

5. Add crabmeat and stir well. Cook for another 5 minutes or until heated through. Sprinkle with paprika and serve hot.

Serves 4 to 6

Pick-a-Pepper Soup
Equatorial Guinea, West Africa

Soups are an important part of West African cuisine and are served for lunch, supper, and sometimes for breakfast. (Recipe by Marcia Vaughan)

1½	cups water
1	pound red snapper fillet, or any white fish fillet, cut into bite-size pieces
3	medium onions, peeled and sliced
2	tomatoes, chopped
1	red bell pepper, seeds removed, chopped
¼	teaspoon cayenne pepper
1	bay leaf
¼	teaspoon dried basil
½	teaspoon salt
½	teaspoon black pepper
½	teaspoon paprika
	pinch dried rosemary
1	tablespoon lemon juice
½	teaspoon vegetable oil

1. Bring the water to a boil in a large pot over high heat.
2. Add all the ingredients except the oil.
3. Cover the pot and simmer over low heat for 1 hour, stirring occasionally. If broth cooks away and the soup starts to get thick and dry, add more water.
4. Add the oil and cook for 5 more minutes. Remove the bay leaf before serving. Serve hot.

Serves 4

West African pick-a-pepper soup (above) is a spicy mix of three kinds of peppers. The recipe for Caribbean-style callaloo (left) is on page 29.

Deep-fried catfish (center) and red beans and rice (left) are crowd pleasers perfect for a Kwanzaa feast. The recipe for red beans and rice is on page 34.

MAIN DISHES
Deep-Fried Catfish
United States

This recipe was created by my dear friend Carolyn, who wanted to prepare catfish, a food long eaten by African Americans, in a healthy way.—A.A.B.

2   pounds catfish fillets
1   cup yellow cornmeal
     pinch seasoning salt
1   teaspoon pepper
1   teaspoon garlic powder
1   cup canola oil
     tabasco sauce or ketchup

1. Trim edges, remove skin from back of fillets, and discard.
2. Mix remaining ingredients, except for oil, in a large, shallow bowl.
3. One by one, coat fish fillets in cornmeal mixture, making sure fish is well covered. Shake excess cornmeal off fish and place fillets on waxed paper.
4. Heat oil in a skillet for 2 to 3 minutes on medium-high heat.
5. Using a spatula, arrange fish fillets in skillet so they do not overlap. Cook until golden brown on bottom, then turn over carefully and brown other side. Cooking time will vary from 5 to 10 minutes, each side, depending on the thickness of the fish. Cooked fish should break off easily in firm chunks when tested with a fork.
6. Remove fillets from skillet and drain excess oil from fish on paper towels. Serve warm, with tabasco sauce or ketchup.

Serves 4 to 6

Red Beans and Rice
United States

My mother, Carole, used to prepare red beans and rice every Friday when I was a child. We would enjoy wiping the bowl with corn bread after the beans were gone. My mother's recipe used pork, but when I became a vegetarian, I created this version.—A.A.B.

1	pound dried red kidney beans
2	quarts water
2	cubes vegetable bouillon
¼	cup chopped white onion
1	clove garlic, peeled and chopped
1	teaspoon crushed bay leaves
3	cups uncooked quick brown rice
	salt and pepper to taste

1. Place beans in a colander and rinse well with cold water.

2. In a large bowl or pot, combine beans with enough water to cover plus one inch. Soak beans overnight or for at least 6 hours.

3. In a large soup pot, bring 2 quarts of water to a boil. Add bouillon cubes and continue to boil for 10 minutes.

4. Drain beans again in colander and add them to boiling water. Cover tightly, lower heat to lowest setting, and simmer for 2 hours. Stir every now and then so beans don't stick to pot.

5. Add onions, garlic, and bay leaves. Cook an additional hour, stirring when necessary—every 15 minutes or more.

6. Prepare rice according to package instructions.

7. When bean broth is slightly thick and cloudy and beans are tender, add salt and pepper to taste. Remove from heat and serve over rice or mix together.

Serves 6 to 10

Hopping John
United States

Hopping John is often served on New Year's Day. The black-eyed peas are for good luck, rice for prosperity, and ham for friendship. (Recipe by Marcia Vaughan)

2	cups dried black-eyed peas
9	cups water, divided
1	pound ham hock
1	large onion, peeled and chopped
1	clove garlic, peeled and minced
1	bay leaf
2	teaspoons dried parsley
¼	teaspoon cayenne pepper
1½	cups uncooked white rice

1. Soak the dried peas overnight in 4 cups water. Drain.

2. Cut off any excess fat from the ham hock. Combine ham hock, 5 cups water, onion, garlic, bay leaf, and parsley in a large saucepan. Bring to a boil over high heat. Reduce heat and simmer, covered, for 1 hour. Stir occasionally.

3. Add the black-eyed peas and cayenne pepper. Continue to simmer, covered, for 30 minutes.

4. Stir in rice and simmer, covered, for 20 minutes or until liquid is absorbed.

5. Remove bay leaf and discard. Remove ham hock with tongs. Cool. Slice ham off bone. Discard bone and any fat.

6. Spread the pea and rice mixture in a shallow serving dish. Top with ham.

Serves 6

Use chapatis (upper left) in place of a fork to pick up chunks of two traditional Ethiopian dishes, luku (left) and meat curry (right). You'll find the recipe for chapatis on page 28 and the recipe for meat curry on page 38.

Luku
Ethiopia

Because of the high cost of chicken in Africa, luku is usually reserved for special occasions or celebrations. (Recipe by Constance Nabwire and Bertha Vining Montgomery)

8	hard-boiled eggs
¾	cup vegetable oil
5 to 6	cups chopped onion
¼	cup tomato paste
½	cup water
2	teaspoons salt
¾	teaspoon black pepper
1¼	tablespoons garlic, peeled and minced
2	teaspoons paprika
¼	teaspoon ground cumin (optional)
8	pieces chicken

1. Remove shells from eggs. With a sharp knife, make 4 to 5 shallow cuts on both sides of each egg. Set aside.
2. In a large kettle, heat 2 tablespoons oil over medium-high heat for 1 minute. Add onions and sauté for 8 to 10 minutes or until onions start to turn brown.
3. Reduce heat to medium and add tomato paste and ½ cup water. Stir well. Cook for 10 minutes, then add remaining oil. Cook for 5 minutes more.
4. Add salt, pepper, garlic, paprika, cumin, and chicken. Reduce heat to low and simmer, uncovered, for about 30 minutes.
5. Add eggs, cover, and cook for 10 minutes or until chicken is tender.

Serves 6

Meat Curry
East Africa

Curries are very popular in East Africa. This dish is sometimes made with lamb or goat instead of chicken. (Recipe by Constance Nabwire and Bertha Vining Montgomery)

½	cup vegetable oil
1	medium onion, chopped
4	cloves garlic, peeled and minced
2	tablespoons prepared curry powder
6	ounces tomato paste
4 to 6	pieces chicken
2	medium white potatoes, peeled and quartered
½	cup fresh coriander

1. In a large frying pan, warm oil over medium heat for 1 minute. Add onion, garlic, and curry powder. Stir well.
2. Stir in tomato paste and cook about 10 minutes or until tomato paste separates from oil. Stir to blend oil and tomato paste.
3. Add chicken, lower heat, and cover. Simmer for 35 minutes.
4. Add potatoes, cover, and simmer 15 minutes or until tender.
5. Add coriander and simmer, uncovered, 10 minutes more.

Serves 4 to 6

Betty's Browned-Down Chicken

Trinidad and Tobago

"Browning down" gives meat a golden brown color and makes a tasty gravy. (Recipe by Cheryl Davidson Kaufman)

3	pounds chicken (about 6 pieces)
2	cloves garlic, peeled and crushed
1	medium onion, peeled and sliced
1	chili, seeded and chopped
1	teaspoon salt
½	teaspoon black pepper
1	teaspoon dried thyme
	dash ground ginger
2	tablespoons apple cider vinegar
1	tablespoon sugar
½	cup vegetable oil

1. Wash chicken and rub with garlic. Place in a large bowl and add onions, chili, salt, pepper, thyme, and ginger. Pour vinegar over chicken, cover tightly, and refrigerate overnight.

2. In a large frying pan, combine sugar and oil. Cook over medium heat, stirring constantly, for 5 minutes or until sugar has dissolved.

3. Scrape onions off chicken. Do not discard onions or vinegar mixture. In the frying pan, brown chicken, a few pieces at a time, turning to brown all sides evenly.

4. Return browned chicken to pan, add onions and vinegar mixture and enough water to almost cover chicken.

5. Cover and cook over medium heat for 30 minutes or until chicken is tender.

Serves 4 to 6

Salad greens (right) make a healthy and colorful addition to any Kwanzaa meal. Other popular vegetable side dishes are honey-glazed sweet potatoes (front left) and steamed kale (back left). The recipe for honey-glazed sweet potatoes is on page 42, while the recipe for steamed kale is on page 43.

VEGETABLES
Mixed Salad Greens with Orange-Lemon Dressing
United States

A salad is an excellent addition to an evening meal. The dressing here is light and gives the greens just a tinge of sweetness.—A.A.B.

1	head red lettuce
1	head romaine lettuce
1 or 2	seedless oranges, peeled and sliced small

DRESSING

½	cup orange juice
¼	cup fresh-squeezed lemon juice
1	tablespoon canola oil
1	teaspoon honey

1. Mix dressing ingredients in a small bowl. Cover and chill in refrigerator for 1 hour.
2. Wash salad greens and drain. Tear greens into bite-size pieces and place in a large salad bowl. Add orange slices.
3. Toss salad greens with dressing, adding just enough dressing to coat. Serve.

Serves 6 to 8

Honey-Glazed Sweet Potatoes

United States

Sweet potatoes were the sweet side dish we wanted at every family gathering. The sight of those orange potatoes, slightly glazed, was a reminder to us that this was a special occasion.—A.A.B.

6 to 8	medium-size sweet potatoes
¾	cup (1½ sticks) butter or margarine
½	cup brown sugar, packed tightly in measuring cup
½	cup honey
1	teaspoon cinnamon
1	teaspoon nutmeg

1. Place sweet potatoes in a large pot and add enough water to barely cover them. Bring water to a boil and cook sweet potatoes 20 to 30 minutes, until they are soft when pierced with a fork.

2. Remove sweet potatoes from hot water and allow to cool in a large bowl for 1 to 2 hours. Once cool, peel off skins and cut potatoes into small chunks.

3. In a saucepan over medium heat, melt butter and then add sugar, honey, cinnamon, and nutmeg. Cook for 10 minutes.

4. Add sweet potatoes. Cook over low heat for about 20 minutes, stirring often so potatoes do not stick to pan. Serve hot.

Serves 8 to 10

Steamed Kale
United States

Steamed kale is a good addition to any meal. It's both healthy and easy to prepare.—A.A.B.

- 1 bunch kale
- ½ cup water
- ½ cup fresh-squeczed lemon juice
- 1 clove garlic, peeled and chopped

1. Wash kale and tear into bite-size pieces.
2. Place kale in a large pot. Add water, lemon juice, and garlic. Bring to a boil, then cover pot, and reduce heat. Simmer until kale is tender, about 30 minutes.
3. Transfer kale to serving dish. Serve with a slotted spoon while warm.

Serves 4

This sweet and spicy corn bread tastes great as a side dish with kale or on its own. The recipe for cornmeal and wheat corn bread is on page 27.

Chandra's peach cobbler—with or without a scoop of ice cream or frozen yogurt
on top—is a tasty dessert for the karamu.

DESSERTS
Chandra's Peach Cobbler
United States

My sister, Chandra, is a woman whose roots lie in southern cooking. This recipe is a tribute to our history.—A.A.B.

2   30-ounce cans peaches
    (Use peaches canned in
    their own juice and not in
    sugar or syrup.)
¾   cup brown sugar, packed
    tightly in measuring cup
2   tablespoons cornstarch
1   teaspoon vanilla extract
¼   teaspoon cinnamon
1   15-ounce package refrigerated
    ready-made pie crust
1   tablespoon butter or
    margarine, cut into
    pea-size pieces

1. Preheat the oven to 400°.
2. Drain the peaches and set aside.

Pour 1½ cups of the juice from the peaches into a saucepan.
3. Add brown sugar and cornstarch to juice. Cook over low heat, stirring until thickened. Stir in vanilla extract and cinnamon. Add peaches and cook for about 5 minutes, or until fruit is hot.
4. Remove from heat and spoon mixture into 9- by 13-inch non-stick pan. The liquid should barely cover the peaches.
5. Spread crust out flat on a piece of waxed paper. Using a table knife, cut dough into strips about 1 inch wide. Lay crust strips vertically and horizontally over fruit mixture. Dot crust with butter and sprinkle lightly with cinnamon.
6. Bake for 30 to 40 minutes, or until crust is golden brown. Allow to cool slightly before serving.

Serves 8 to 10

Baked Plantain on the Shell

East and West Africa

Here's a way to enjoy plantain, a starchy fruit similar to a banana, and satisfy your sweet tooth. (Recipe by Constance Nabwire and Bertha Vining Montgomery)

4 large, ripe plantains
½ cup brown sugar
¾ teaspoon cinnamon
¼ cup butter or margarine, melted

1. Preheat oven to 350°.
2. Wash plantains and cut in half lengthwise. Do not peel.
3. Arrange in a shallow baking dish with the cut sides facing up.
4. In a small bowl, combine brown sugar, cinnamon, and melted butter. Stir well.

5. Top plantains with brown sugar mixture.
6. Cover pan with foil and bake for 35 minutes or until plantains are soft.

Serves 4

African desserts usually have just a touch of sweetness. Baked plantain (left) and sweet balls (right) are typical desserts from across the continent of Africa.

Sweet Balls
Ghana

These little doughnuts are best when they are still warm. (Recipe by Constance Nabwire and Bertha Vining Montgomery)

1	egg
½	teaspoon salt
3	teaspoons baking powder
1½	cups sugar
½	teaspoon nutmeg
1½	cups warm water
3¾ to 4¼	cups all-purpose flour
	vegetable oil

1. In a large bowl, combine egg, salt, baking powder, sugar, and nutmeg and stir well. Add 1½ cups warm water and stir again.
2. Gradually stir in enough flour so that dough is stiff and only slightly sticky.
3. With clean, floured hands, roll dough into balls the size of walnuts.
4. Pour ½ inch oil into pan and heat over medium-high heat for 4 to 5 minutes.
5. Carefully place balls in oil, a few at a time, and fry 3 or 4 minutes per side or until golden brown. Remove from pan with slotted spoon and drain on paper towel. Serve warm.

Makes 25 to 30 doughnuts

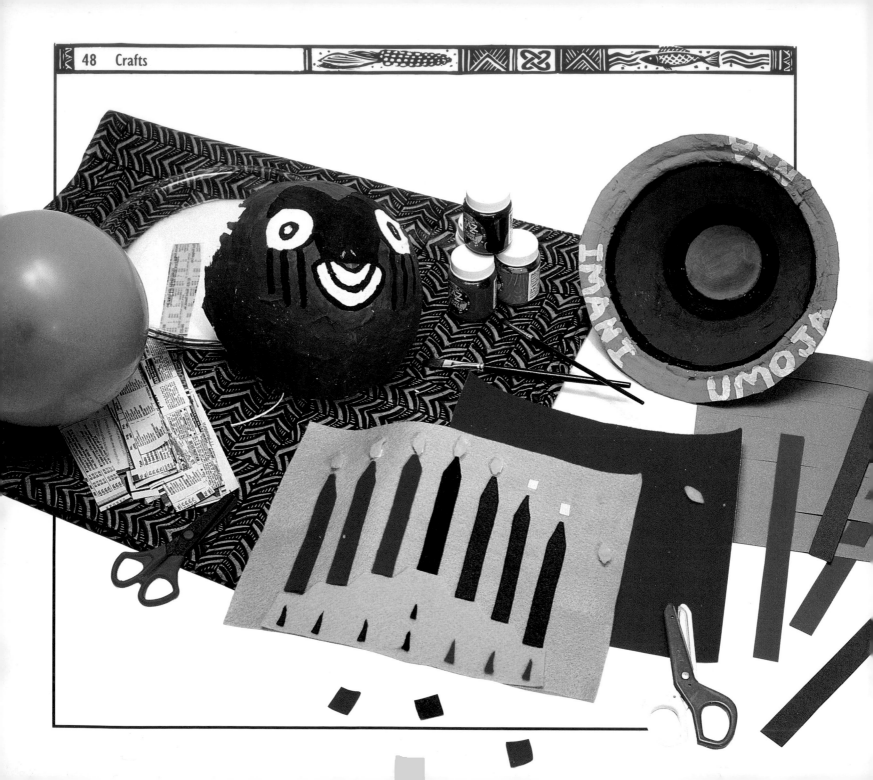

CRAFTS

 Celebrating Kwanzaa
allows us to show our
creativity. We can show
our talents and commemorate
Kwanzaa at the same time by
making crafts. Kwanzaa is a holiday based upon giving, sharing,
and remembering our relatives,
both past and present.

On the pages that follow, you'll
find instructions for making a
mkeka, kinara tapestry, bowl,
mask, African headdress, and skirt.
I hope you enjoy making them
and celebrating Kwanzaa. You can
use these crafts throughout the
year whenever family and friends
come together to celebrate African-
American culture and history.

Before You Begin

Getting ready to make crafts is a
lot like getting ready to cook. Take
a look at the list of materials need-
ed for each craft before you begin.
Then read the instructions from
start to finish. Some crafts on the
pages that follow take more time
to make than others, so plan
ahead. In a few cases, you will
need to ask a grown-up to help
you. If you want to start with
something you can do on your
own, try the mkeka or the African
headdress.

Mkeka

To make a woven mat, you will need:

- 3 to 4 rectangular sheets of 12- by 9-inch construction paper in different colors
- ruler
- pencil
- scissors
- glue (optional)

1. Fold one sheet of paper in half so it measures 6 by 9 inches. Place a ruler next to the fold and use your pencil to mark along the fold every inch. Do the same on the opposite edge. Then draw lines joining the opposite pencil marks.

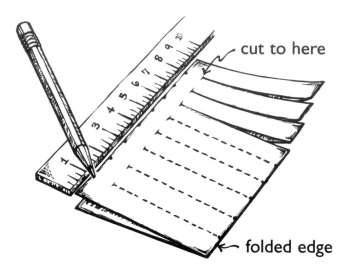

cut to here

folded edge

Cut through both thicknesses of paper along the pencil lines from the fold to about 1 inch from the unfolded edges. Unfold the sheet and set aside.

2. Take the other sheets of paper and cut them into 1-inch-wide strips that are 9 inches long.

3. Now choose one of the strips and weave it in and out of the cuts you made in the first sheet of paper. Pull the woven strip snugly to one end of the larger sheet.

Choose a strip of another color to weave in next. Pull it snugly next to the first strip.

4. Continue weaving in strips, alternating colors, until there is no more room on the larger sheet of paper. You can either glue down ends to secure them or leave as is.

Note: You can use lengths of braided rope, colored yarn, or ribbon to make a mkeka, too. Cut 12-inch lengths and weave them together as shown below. To bind the ends, glue them down or take a large darning needle and heavy thread. Sew along the edges of the mkeka.

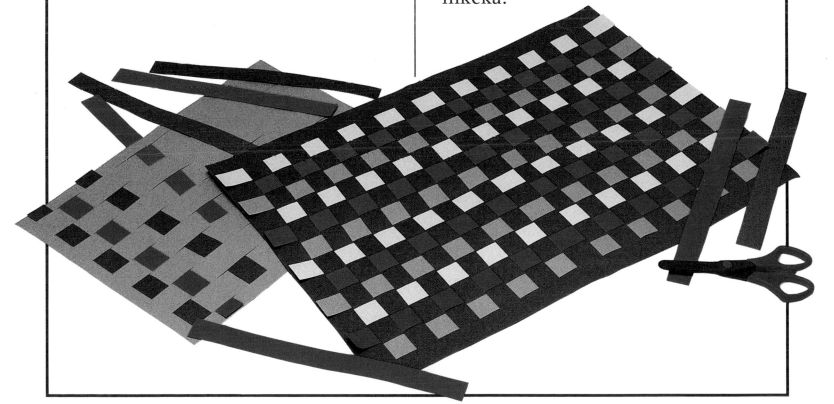

Kinara Tapestry

To make a kinara tapestry to pin to your wall, you will need:

scissors

rectangles of felt in five colors (red, black, green, gold, and another color of your choice)

tracing paper

pencil

glue

velcro fasteners (optional)

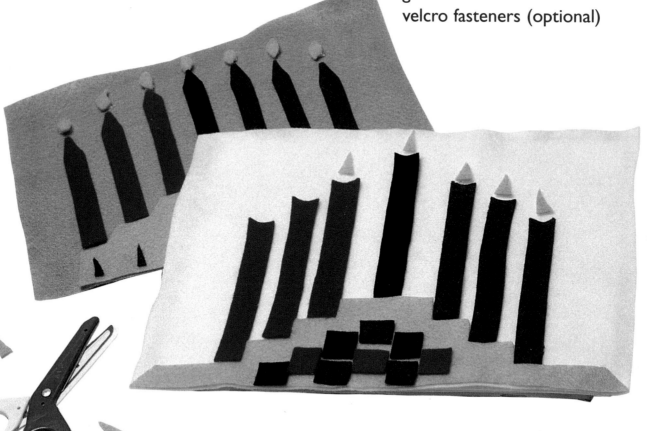

1. Cut out candle shapes from the green, red, and black pieces of felt. If you want to use a pattern, place tracing paper on top of figure A on page 54 and trace. Cut out tracing paper pattern. Place the pattern on top of the felt and trace around it. Then cut along the lines. You'll need three red candles, three green candles, and one black candle.

2. Now cut out a candleholder shape from the gold piece of felt. Use figure B on page 54 as a pattern or create your own kinara shape. Make sure that the middle of your candleholder is higher than the rest so that the middle candle will be the highest of the candle shapes. Set aside the extra pieces of felt.

3. Take the fifth piece of felt and lay it flat. This will be the background color and the base for your tapestry. Lay the kinara and candle pieces on the base. Make sure the black candle is in the middle, with the red candles on the left side and the green candles on the right side. Carefully glue down each piece. You probably won't need more than a few drops of glue on each piece.

4. From the extra gold felt, cut out seven teardrop shapes. You can use figure C on page 54 as a pattern. These teardrop shapes will be the flames for your candles.

5. Pin your kinara tapestry to the wall. As you celebrate each day of Kwanzaa, add a flame to a candle. Felt usually sticks to itself, but if your flames don't stick well enough, attach velcro to their backs and to the background.

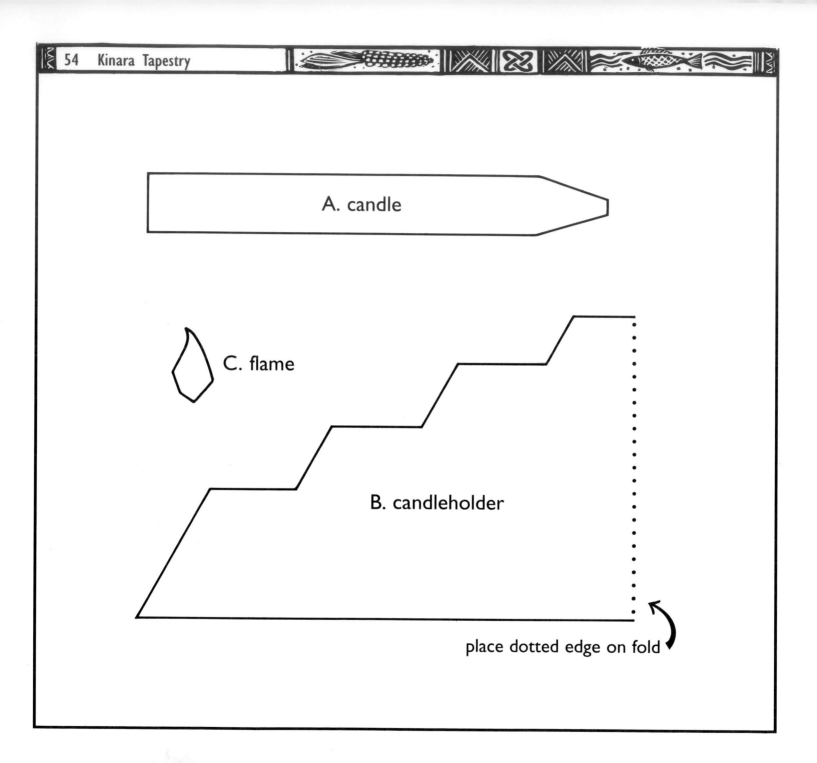

A. candle

C. flame

B. candleholder

place dotted edge on fold

African Bowl or Mask

These projects involve papier-mâché, which can be messy. Be sure to ask an adult for help. And be sure to clean up well after you're done. To make a bowl or mask, you will need:

> a shallow dish
> flour
> water
> balloon or bowl
> petroleum jelly
> strips of newspaper or other waste-paper (such as computer paper, paper bags, and discarded envelopes)
> a cup
> table knife or thin spatula
> tempera paints
> paintbrushes
> scissors
> sharp knife (for mask)

1. In the shallow dish, mix flour and water into a paste. Use 1 part flour to 1 part water. For example, mix 1 cup water into 1 cup flour. Stir well to remove lumps.
2. To make a mold, blow up a balloon and tie the end closed. Or cover a bowl with a layer of petroleum jelly, applying more around the rim of the bowl. (This will keep your papier-mâché from sticking permanently to the bowl.)
3. Tear or cut the wastepaper into long strips, then into shorter bits about 1 inch wide and 3 inches long.
4. Prepare a work surface by covering a table with newspapers. Invert the bowl onto the work surface. Or, if you are using a balloon, set it tied-end-down into a cup. (This will prevent the balloon from rolling around too much.)

5. Dip strips of paper in the paste, covering each side with a thin layer of paste. Then lay the strips sticky-side-down onto your mold. Start at the top and work down, being sure to overlap the strips. Wipe off any big, thick globs of paste, so the papier-mâché dries evenly. Once you have an even layer of strips, repeat. Keep on layering until the papier-mâché is five layers thick.

6. Let dry completely (at least overnight). Carefully separate the papier-mâché from the bowl by slipping in a table knife or thin spatula to loosen. Remove as much of the petroleum jelly from the papier-mâché as you can. If the petroleum jelly doesn't come off, add a thin layer of flour and water to the inside and allow to dry. (This will help your paints adhere.) To separate the papier-mâché from the balloon, simply pop the balloon and pull out the balloon pieces. Trim any rough edges with scissors.

To make a bowl, use tempera paint and paintbrushes to cover the inside and outside. Create your own designs or look in books about Africa for African designs you can use. If you don't want to paint your bowl, cut out bits of colored construction paper or magazine pictures of famous African Americans. Use a thin layer of flour-and-water paste to attach the paper or pictures to the outside of your bowl.

To make a mask, you can paint a face on the outside. Trim the edges with scissors to fit the mask to the shape of your head. If you want to wear the mask, hold the unpainted papier-mâché to your face and use a pencil to mark where your eyes and mouth will fit. Ask an adult to use a sharp knife to cut eye and mouth holes on the inside of the mask and to cut holes at each side for string ties. Now paint as directed above.

African Headdress and Skirt

Many times during the Kwanzaa celebration, men, women, and children dress in African clothing. Young girls and women can join in the festivities by creating a head-dress and skirt from African fabric.

To make a headdress, you'll need 2 yards of fabric, folded or cut to a width of about 1 foot. Wrap it around your head like a scarf, bringing the ends together in the back. Twist the ends of the fabric as you continue to wrap them around your head. When you come to the end of the fabric, tuck the ends under the fabric already wrapped around your head.

To cover your body in African cloth, take enough African fabric to fit around your hips at least two times. When held around your hips, the fabric should be long enough to extend from your waist to your toes, with more to spare.

Wrap the fabric around your body twice, knotting it at the side. Roll the waistband down until you've made a skirt. Under this you can wear a bodysuit or leotard. Now you have a unique African outfit!

Nguzo Saba: The Seven Principles

by Maulana Karenga

Umoja (Unity)
To strive for and maintain unity in the family, community, nation, and race.

Kujichagulia (Self-Determination)
To define ourselves, name ourselves, create for ourselves, and speak for ourselves, instead of being defined, named, created for, and spoken for by others.

Ujima (Collective Work and Responsibility)
To build and maintain our community together, and make our sisters' and brothers' problems our problems; and to solve our problems together.

Ujamaa (Cooperative Economics)
To build and maintain our own stores, shops, and other businesses, and to profit from them together.

Nia (Purpose)
To make our collective vocation the building and developing of our community, in order to restore our people to their traditional greatness.

Kuumba (Creativity)
To do always as much as we can, in the way we can, in order to leave our community more beautiful and beneficial than we inherited it.

Imani (Faith)
To believe with all our hearts in our people, our parents, our teachers, our leaders, and the righteousness and victory of our struggle.

Words for Kwanzaa

Many of the words used at Kwanzaa time come from Swahili, also called Kiswahili.

bendera (behn-DEH-rah): A flag for African Americans

Harambee! (hah-rahm-BEH): Let's pull together!

imani (ee-MAH-nee): Faith

karamu (kah-RAH-moo): The feast

kikombe cha umoja (kee-KOM-beh chah oo-MOH-jah): The unity cup

kinara (kee-NAH-rah): The candleholder

kujichagulia (koo-ji-chah-goo-LEE-ah): Self-determination

kuumba (koo-OOM-bah): Creativity

Kwanzaa (KWAHN-zah): An African-American holiday

mazao (mah-ZAH-oh): The fruits and vegetables

mishumaa saba (mee-shoo-MAH SAH-bah): The seven candles

mkeka (mm-KEH-kah): The mat

muhindi (moo-HIN-dee): The corn

nguzo saba (nn-GOO-zoh SAH-bah): The seven principles behind Kwanzaa

nia (NEE-ah): Purpose

Swahili (swah-HEE-lee), also called **Kiswahili (ki-swah-HEE-lee):** A language of East Africa

ujamaa (oo-jah-MAH): Sharing our work and sharing the profits from our work

ujima (oo-JEE-mah): Working together to achieve success

umoja (oo-MOH-jah): Unity

zawadi (zah-WAH-dee): The gifts

Index

(Recipes and crafts indicated by **bold** type)

Africa, 8, 9, 10, 12, 57, 58, 59
ants-on-a-log, 22, 24, **25**

baked plantain on the shell, **46**
beans: hopping John, 24, **35;**
    red beans and rice, 32, **34**
bendera (African-American
    flag), 9, 61
Betty's browned-down chicken,
    21, **39**
bowl, African, 49, **55–57**
breads: chapatis, **28,** 36; corn-
    meal and wheat corn bread,
    27, 43; hush puppies, 24, **26**

callaloo, **29,** 31
candleholder. *See* kinara
candles. *See* mishumaa
catfish, deep-fried, 32, **33**
chapatis, **28,** 36
chicken: Betty's browned-down
    chicken, 21, **39;** luku, 36, **37;**
    meat curry, 36, **38**
cobbler, Chandra's peach, 44, **45**
cooking: cleaning up after, 23;
    importance in African-
    American families, 21; prepa-
    ration for, 22; safety, 22–23;
    terms, 23
corn, ears of. *See* muhindi
cornmeal and wheat corn
    bread, **27,** 43

cup. *See* kikombe
curry, meat, 36, **38**

deep-fried catfish, 32, **33**
desserts: baked plantain on the
    shell, **46;** Chandra's peach
    cobbler, 44, **45;** sweet balls,
    46, **47**

fish: deep-fried catfish, 32, **33;**
    pick-a-pepper soup, **30,** 31
flag. *See* bendera
fruits and vegetables. *See*
    mazao

gifts. *See* zawadi
greens: callaloo, **29,** 31; mixed
    salad greens with orange-
    lemon dressing, 22, 40, **41;**
    steamed kale, 40, **43**

harambee, 14, 19, 61
headdress, African, 49, **58**
honey-glazed sweet potatoes,
    40, **42**
hopping John, 24, **35**
hush puppies, 24, **26**

imani (faith), 13, 19, 20, 60, 61

kale, steamed, 40, **43**
karamu, 17, 18, 61
Karenga, Maulana: creation of
    Kwanzaa and, 7, 8–9, 10;
    nguzo saba (seven principles)
    and, 13, 20, 60

Karenga, Tiamoyo, 8
kikombe cha umoja (unity
    cup), 11, 12, 14, 15, 17, 18,
    19, 61
kinara (candleholder), 10, 12,
    13, 17, 19, 61
kinara tapestry, 49, **52–54**
Kiswahili. *See* Swahili
kujichagulia (self-determina-
    tion), 13, 14–15, 16, 20, 60,
    61
kuumba (creativity), 13, 17, 18,
    19, 20, 60, 61
Kwanzaa: colors of, 9, 10, 17;
    creation of, 7, 8–9; defined,
    7, 12, 61; principles of, 7,
    13–20, 60; religion and, 12,
    13, 19; symbols of, 9–11;
    when celebrated, 7, 12

luku, 36, **37**

main dishes: Betty's browned-
    down chicken, 21, **39;** deep-
    fried catfish, 32, **33;** hopping
    John, 24, **35;** luku, 36, **37;**
    meat curry, 36, **38;** red beans
    and rice, 32, **34**
mask, African, 49, **55–57**
mat. *See* mkeka
mazao (fruits and vegetables),
    10, 12, 17, 61
meat curry, 36, **38**
mishumaa saba (seven can-
    dles), 10, 12, 13, 14, 15, 16,
    17, 19, 61